the best of BARBERSHOP

CONTENTS

AIN'T WE GOT FUN 22

BABY FACE 26

CALIFORNIA HERE I COME 3

CAROLINA IN THE MORNING 32

CHINATOWN, MY CHINATOWN 15

(Kentucky's Way Of Sayin') GOOD MORNING 35

I'M FOREVER BLOWING BUBBLES 20

IN THE SHADE OF THE OLD APPLE TREE 38

I WISH I HAD MY OLD GAL BACK 6

LET THE REST OF THE WORLD GO BY 30

MEMORIES 16

MOONLIGHT BAY 8

MY BUDDY 25

NELLIE DEAN 29

PRETTY BABY 10

SMILES 34

THE SUNSHINE OF YOUR SMILE 12

SWEET ADELINE 18

TILL WE MEET AGAIN 40

YOUR EYES HAVE TOLD ME SO 39

CALIFORNIA
Here I Come

Arranged by
DALE STEVENS

Words and Music by
AL JOLSON, BUD DeSYLVA
and JOSEPH MEYER

I WISH I HAD MY OLD GAL BACK AGAIN

Words and Music by
JACK YELLEN, MILTON AGER and LEW POLLACK
Arranged by
Arranging Class Harmony Education Program, SPEBSQSA, Inc.

MOONLIGHT BAY

Words by
EDWARD MADDEN

Music by
PERCY WENRICH
Arranged by
CHARLES M. MERRILL

PRETTY BABY

Words by
GUS KAHN

Music by
TONY JACKSON and EGBERT VAN ALSTYNE
Arranged by
CHARLES M. MERRILL

INTRODUCTION

Rock - a - bye, ba - by, on the tree - top,

when the wind blows, the cra - dle will rock. Ev - 'ry -

REFRAIN

bod - y loves a ba - by that's why I'm in love with you, Pret - ty

Ba - by, Pret - ty Ba - by;___ And I'd like to be your sis - ter, broth - er,

Boom

THE SUNSHINE OF YOUR SMILE

Words by
LEONARD COOKE

Music by
LILLIAN RAY
Arranged by
WILLIS A. DIEKEMA

14

CHINATOWN, MY CHINATOWN

Words by
WILLIAM JEROME

Music by
JEAN SCHWARTZ
Arranged by
MAURICE E. REAGAN and S.S.

MEMORIES

Words by
GUS KAHN

Music by
EGBERT VAN ALSTYNE
Arranged by
The 1964 H.E.P. Advanced Arrangers Class

VERSE

Round me at twi-light come steal-ing,— Shad-ows of days that are gone.—

Dreams of the old days re-veal-ing — Mem-'ries of Love's gold-en dawn.———

gold-en dawn.

CHORUS

so true.

Mem - o - ries, Mem - o - ries, *Melody* Dreams of love so true.——— *Melody*

Dreams of love so true.——

to you.

O'er the sea of Mem-o-ry I'm drift-ing back to you.———

to you.

to you.

Child-hood days, wild-wood days, a - mong the birds and bees;___ You

left me a-lone, But still you're my own, In my beau-ti-ful

Mem - o - ries, Mem - o - ries, Dreams of love so true.___ You

left me a-lone, But still you're my own, In my beau-ti-ful Mem - o - ries.___

Mem - o - ries.

SWEET ADELINE
(You're The Flower Of My Heart, Sweet Adeline)

Words by
RICHARD H. GERARD

Music by
HARRY ARMSTRONG
Arranged by
SIGMUND SPAETH

I'M FOREVER BLOWING BUBBLES

Words and Music by
JAAN KENBROVIN and JOHN WILLIAM KELLETTE
Arranged by
PHIL EMBURY

REFRAIN

I'm for-ev-er blow-ing bub-bles, bub - bles, Pret - ty bub-bles

in the air, in the air_____ They fly so high, near-ly reach the

sky, Then like my dreams they fade and die. For-tune's al - ways

hid-ing (hid-ing), I've looked ev-'ry-where;__ I'm for-ev-er

(Hm)__

blow-ing bub-bles,__ Pret-ty bub-bles in the air.__

(Hm)__

(Hm)__

AIN'T WE GOT FUN

Arranged by
BOB MEYER

Words and Music by
GUS KAHN, RAYMOND B. EGAN
and RICHARD A. WHITING

Don't wash the dish - es   Just throw them a - way.

In the win - ter,   In the sum - mer,   Don't we have a lot of

Melody

In ___   And in ___   Oh, don't ___

fun.   Times are bum and   Get - ting bum - mer

Yes a lot of fun and Times ___   Get - ting

Still we have fun.   There's noth-ing sur - er, The

There's

rich get rich and the poor get chil - dren.   In the mean-time,   In be - tween time,

In ___   And in ___

Ain't we got,   In the mean-time, In be - tween time, Ain't We Got Fun. ___

Fun.

MY BUDDY

Words by
GUS KAHN

Music by
WALTER DONALDSON
Arranged by
MAURICE E. REAGAN and S.S.

BABY FACE

Arranged by
DAVE STEVENS

Words and Music by
BENNY DAVIS and HARRY AKST

NELLIE DEAN
(You're My Heart's Desire, I Love You, Nellie Dean)

Music by
HARRY ARMSTRONG
Arranged by
SIGMUND SPAETH

Words by
RICHARD H. GERARD

LET THE REST OF THE WORLD GO BY

Music by
ERNEST R. BALL
Arranged by
The Advanced Arranging Class,
Harmony Education Program, SPEBSQSA, Inc.

Words by
J.K. BRENNAN

CAROLINA IN THE MORNING

Words by
GUS KAHN

Music by
WALTER DONALDSON
Arranged by
SIGMUND SPAETH

SMILES

Words by
J. WILL CALLAHAN

Music by
LEE S. ROBERTS
Arranged by
SIGMUND SPAETH

Kentucky's Way of Sayin'
"GOOD MORNIN'"

Words by
GUS KAHN

Music by
EGBERT VAN ALSTYNE
Arranged by
SHERRY BROWN

INTRO.

That's old Ken-tuck-y's way of say-in' "Good Morn - - in'," Yes sir!

VERSE

I like the folks who say "Hel - lo"_____ In such a way they let you
(hel-lo)

(they're glad to see you)

know __ they're glad to see you back a - gain, _ and they'll hate to see _ you
(they're glad to see you)

(see you go)
go. I like the folks who say "Good-Bye"_____ with just a lit-tle heart-felt
(good-bye)
(see you go)

sigh.— But most of all I like the way — Ken-tuck-y greets each

(but most of all I)

CHORUS

new-born day:— "Good Morn-in'" the bees are hum-min', "Morn-in'" a

(Bm) (Bm)

new day com-in', "Morn-in'" your heart's drum, drum-min' wake up, ——— and see the

(Bm) (wake up, wake up)

sun-beams that come a-peep-in' say-in' "no time for sleep-in'."

(Bm) (Bm)

Get out and set out to wan-der those hills out yon-der.

(Bm) (Bm)

IN THE SHADE OF THE OLD APPLE TREE

Words by
HARRY H. WILLIAMS

Music by
EGBERT VAN ALSTYNE
Arranged by
FRANK H. THORNE

YOUR EYES HAVE TOLD ME SO

Words by
GUS KAHN and EGBERT VAN ALSTYNE

Music by
WALTER BLAUFUSS
Arranged by
FRANK H. THORNE

TILL WE MEET AGAIN

Words by
RAYMOND B. EGAN

Music by
RICHARD A. WHITING
Arranged by
PHIL EMBURY